CALM WEALTH: A PRACTICAL GUIDE TO DOL-LAR-COST AVERAGING ETFS

CALM WEALTH

A PRACTICAL GUIDE TO DOLLAR-COST AVERAGING ETFS

ANDRAS M.NAGY

ISBN: 978-1-968194-18-5

Contents

Chapter 1

The Essence of Dollar-Cost Averaging

Most people approach investing with the same emotions they bring to a casino — excitement, fear, and a secret hope to walk away richer by the end of the night. Markets rise, and everyone feels brilliant. Markets fall, and suddenly everyone is a philosopher, wondering why they didn't see it coming. The cycle repeats endlessly, chewing up both amateurs and professionals alike.

There's a better way. It doesn't require predicting anything, timing anything, or even being particularly clever. It just requires patience and discipline — two traits that most investors underestimate because they sound too simple to be powerful.

That approach is called dollar-cost averaging, or DCA. It's the habit of investing a fixed amount of money at regular intervals, no matter what the market is doing. You buy when prices are high, you buy when prices are low, and over time, you average your way into the market at a fair and balanced cost.

It's not about catching the top or bottom — it's about building steadily, in both wealth and peace of mind.

THE CALM IN CONSISTENCY

Imagine you have $10,000 to invest.

Most people are tempted to drop it all into the market at once, hoping prices go up right after. But what if they don't? What if the next month brings a correction? Suddenly your $10,000 investment is worth $8,500, and panic sets in. You start to question your judgment. Maybe you think about selling — or you stop investing altogether for months, waiting for "clarity" that never arrives.

Now, instead, imagine dividing that same $10,000 into 10 equal parts — $1,000 a month over 10 months.

When the market is up, your $1,000 buys fewer shares. When it's down, it buys more. Over time, this smooths out your entry price. You don't have to time the market; you simply participate in it. You let the natural volatility of prices work for you, not against you.

Let's make this real with a simple example.

Month	Share Price	Amount Invested	Shares Purchased	Total Shares
1	$100	$1,000	10.00	10.00
2	$90	$1,000	11.11	21.11
3	$80	$1,000	12.50	33.61
4	$85	$1,000	11.76	45.37
5	$95	$1,000	10.53	55.90
6	$100	$1,000	10.00	65.90
7	$110	$1,000	9.09	74.99
8	$105	$1,000	9.52	84.51
9	$90	$1,000	11.11	95.62
10	$100	$1,000	10.00	105.62

After 10 months, you've invested $10,000 total. Your average cost per share is about $94.70, even though prices ranged from $80 to $110.

If you had invested the full $10,000 at the start when shares were $100, you'd have 100 shares worth $10,000.
But with DCA, you end up with 105.62 shares — worth $10,562 if the price ends at $100.

That extra $562 didn't come from luck or prediction. It came from discipline — from showing up consistently while others hesitated.

Investing success is far more about behavior than intelligence.
The smartest analysts and economists often fail not because their data is wrong, but because they can't control their impulses.

Dollar-cost averaging builds behavioral armor. It forces you to invest through both sunshine and storms. You stop asking, "Is now a good time to invest?" and instead remind yourself, "Now is always a good time to invest something."

You remove emotion from the process — and that's where the real magic begins.

Volatility: The Gift Nobody Wants

When markets get turbulent and headlines scream about chaos, most investors freeze. But if you're dollar-cost averaging, you're actually cheering quietly inside. Because every drop in price is an opportunity to buy more at a discount.

This is the paradox of the calm investor: volatility feels uncomfortable, but it's the very thing that builds long-term wealth.

In later chapters, we'll refine this idea even more — by using volatility itself (measured by the VIX index) to guide how much you invest at a given time.

For now, just understand this: every market downturn plants the seeds of future gains, and dollar-cost averaging makes sure you're always there to collect the harvest.

SLEEPING AT NIGHT

The real test of any investment strategy isn't in bull markets. It's in how well you sleep when the market drops 20%.

DCA offers something priceless — emotional predictability. You don't have to worry about perfect timing or short-term noise. You know your plan: invest regularly, no matter what. Over months and years, the market's natural growth and your steady participation work together quietly in your favor.

The investor who sleeps best isn't the one with the most aggressive portfolio — it's the one with a process they trust.

Where We Go From Here

You've just seen how DCA takes the randomness of markets and turns it into rhythm.

In the next chapter, we'll explore ETFs — the simple, low-cost building blocks that make this strategy easy to apply. Then, we'll take it further by introducing the idea of Dynamic DCA, where you don't just invest regularly — you invest more when fear is high and less when the crowd gets greedy.

That's how you turn uncertainty into opportunity — and how your

$10,000 today becomes the foundation of calm, confident wealth tomorrow.

Chapter 2

The Power of ETFs

If dollar-cost averaging is the rhythm of calm investing, then ETFs are the instruments that play the music.

They don't make a lot of noise. They don't promise overnight riches. But they do something much better — they quietly capture the long-term growth of the world's greatest companies, with very little cost or complexity.

And that's exactly what you want when you're building wealth that lasts.

The Beauty of Simplicity

The modern investor has an almost infinite menu of options — individual stocks, crypto, mutual funds, options, futures, and all sorts of exotic financial inventions. But here's the truth most professionals won't tell you: you don't need any of that to build a serious portfolio.

A handful of well-chosen ETFs (Exchange-Traded Funds) can give you everything you need — global diversification, low fees, transparency, and liquidity.

Each ETF is like a basket of assets. Instead of buying hundreds of individual companies, you buy one ETF that already holds them all. You're instantly diversified — across sectors, geographies, and even asset classes — with a single purchase.

When you combine that with dollar-cost averaging, you create a portfolio that practically manages itself.

Why ETFs Work So Well with Dollar-Cost Averaging

ETFs trade on the stock market like ordinary shares, so you can invest daily, weekly, or monthly — however you prefer. Some platforms make it easy to automate small recurring purchases.

There are no minimums, no complicated paperwork, and no sales commissions (in most cases). You can literally buy $10 worth of an ETF on your lunch break.

Every time you invest — whether the market is up or down — you're adding a little bit more ownership in that basket of companies. Over time, it's not the amount you invest that matters most; it's the consistency with which you do it.

And because ETFs naturally rebalance themselves (companies enter and leave the index automatically), you don't have to constantly worry about managing or trading. You just keep buying, quietly, like a farmer planting seeds every season.

The 3–4 ETFs That Are Enough for Life

Let's talk about the practical side. You mentioned the truth that most investors eventually discover: you only need 3–4 ETFs to build a complete portfolio.

Here's a sample setup that's simple, balanced, and timeless — available through Vanguard, Schwab, or Fidelity:

U.S. Total Stock Market ETF

Examples: VTI (Vanguard), SCHB (Schwab), ITOT (iShares)

This gives you exposure to the entire U.S. market — from giants like Apple and Microsoft to small, fast-growing innovators.

Think of it as your portfolio's beating heart.

International Stock Market ETF

Examples: VXUS (Vanguard), IXUS (iShares), SCHF (Schwab)

The world doesn't end at the U.S. border. This fund captures companies across Europe, Asia, and emerging markets.

It's your ticket to global growth.

Bond Market ETF

Examples: BND (Vanguard), AGG (iShares), SCHZ (Schwab)

Bonds add stability. They act as shock absorbers when stocks stumble.

They won't make you rich, but they'll help you stay rich.

Optional: Real Estate or Dividend ETF

Examples: VNQ (Vanguard Real Estate), SCHD (Schwab Dividend Equity)

These add income and a touch of inflation protection.

Optional — great if you want to balance growth with cash flow.

That's it. Four ETFs, or even just three if you prefer simplicity. No trading, no guessing, no complicated forecasts.

Your only job is to keep investing — calmly, regularly, and automatically.

A $10,000 Example: The Quiet Power of a Balanced Portfolio

Let's take your $10,000 again and spread it across these ETFs:

$4,000 → Total U.S. Stock Market ETF

$3,000 → International Stock Market ETF

$2,000 → Bond Market ETF

$1,000 → Dividend or Real Estate ETF

Now, imagine you invest this not all at once, but through dollar-cost averaging — say, $1,000 a month for 10 months.

Each month, you add to these ETFs in proportion. When the stock market dips, your $400 into the U.S. ETF buys more shares. When international markets lag, your $300 stretches further. When volatility spikes and the VIX rises, you might even increase your daily or weekly buy slightly, as you'll learn in the next chapter.

Over a few years, this steady, automated rhythm builds wealth quietly in the background.

It's not flashy. It's not exciting. But it's powerful.

This is how real wealth accumulates — through patience, process, and peace of mind.

Why 3–4 ETFs Are Enough

When you own total-market ETFs, you're not just buying companies — you're buying entire economies.

In one trade, you hold stakes in thousands of firms: tech giants, energy producers, healthcare innovators, financial institutions, and manufacturers. You don't need to guess which will win — because over time, the market itself rewards productivity, innovation, and human progress.

ETFs make you a silent partner in all of it.

And the fewer moving parts your portfolio has, the fewer chances you have to second-guess yourself. Complexity breeds confusion; simplicity builds conviction.

A Mindset Shift: From Trader to Owner

When you own ETFs, you're not speculating — you're owning slices of real businesses.

Think of it like owning farmland. You wouldn't sell your field every time the weather changed. You plant, you water, and you wait for the harvest.

Dollar-cost averaging through ETFs works the same way.
You invest a little every day, week, or month. You don't care if the price is $100 or $90 or $110. You're building ownership, not chasing prices.

That's how you move from being a nervous trader to a calm, confident owner.

The Peace Dividend of Simplicity

There's a quiet joy that comes from looking at your investment plan and realizing it's beautifully boring.

No frantic decision-making. No emotional roller coasters. Just clear rules, a few excellent ETFs, and a steady flow of contributions that you can slightly adjust when volatility spikes.

The market can do whatever it wants — you already know what you're going to do.

That's freedom.

Next: Using Volatility to Your Advantage

So far, we've built the foundation:

Dollar-cost averaging as your system.

ETFs as your simple, powerful tools.

In the next chapter, we'll go deeper into the one signal that tells you when the market is giving you a sale — volatility, measured by the VIX.

You'll learn exactly how to increase your investment amount when fear spikes — and how to scale it back when the market grows complacent.

Because the calm investor doesn't run from volatility — they use it.

Chapter 3

Market Volatility and the VIX

The word volatility tends to make investors nervous.

It sounds like chaos — wild price swings, panicked headlines, and the feeling that the market's lost its mind. But once you understand what volatility really means — and how to measure it — you'll start to see it as something entirely different: a signal, not a threat.

Volatility tells you when the crowd is fearful. And when fear rises, value quietly appears.

Understanding Volatility: The Market's Emotional Pulse

Every day, prices move up and down. Sometimes gently, like waves on a calm lake. Other times violently, like a stormy sea. This movement — the degree to which prices fluctuate — is what we call volatility.

High volatility means investors are uncertain and emotional. Low volatility means investors feel safe and complacent.

Volatility doesn't tell you where the market is going next — it tells you how intensely people feel about where it's been. It's the emotional pulse of the financial system.

And like any emotional state, it can swing too far in either direction.

Meet the VIX: The "Fear Index"

Volatility has a number — and it's called the VIX.

The VIX, or Volatility Index, was created by the Chicago Board Options Exchange (CBOE). It measures the market's expectation of volatility over the next 30 days, based on options prices for the S&P 500.

Think of it as a forecast of fear.

When the VIX is around 12–18, investors are calm, maybe even a bit overconfident.

Between 20–25, the market's a little uneasy — normal levels of uncertainty.

Between 28–32, investors are getting anxious.

Above 38, fear is spreading.

At 48–52 or higher, we're in full-blown panic mode.

During crises like 2008 or March 2020, the VIX has spiked to 60–80. Those moments feel terrifying. But for the calm investor, they are golden opportunities.

What Volatility Really Means for You

Here's a simple truth:
Volatility is the price of admission for long-term returns.

If markets were perfectly stable, returns would be tiny. Risk and reward are inseparable. Every dip, correction, or crash you endure as an investor is the toll you pay for the privilege of long-term growth.

But most people pay that toll emotionally. They panic, sell low, and buy back high later — transferring wealth from the impatient to the patient.

You, on the other hand, are learning to do something different. You're going to use volatility to your advantage.

Turning Fear Into a Buying Signal

Here's where the dynamic in Dynamic Dollar-Cost Averaging (D-DCA) comes in.

Traditional DCA says, "Just invest the same amount regularly." That's good — it removes emotion and builds discipline.

But you can go one step further. You can use volatility as a guide for how much to invest at any given time.

Think of it like tuning a sailboat — adjusting your sails depending on the strength of the wind. The wind, in this case, is the VIX.

The Dynamic DCA Formula

Here's a practical rule of thumb to apply:

VIX Range	Market Emotion	Action	Example (Daily Buy = $100)
12–25	Calm, normal	Invest your base amount	$100
28–32	Fear rising	Increase by +50%	$150
38–42	Panic growing	Double your buy	$200
48–52	Extreme fear	Increase to 2.5×	$250
60+	Full-blown crisis	Max allocation if funds allow	$300+
When fear subsides	Calm returns	Scale back proportionally	Back to $100

In other words, when the market is frothy and complacent, you stick to your normal plan — no rush. But when fear hits and volatility spikes, you lean in.

You're not guessing when the bottom will arrive — you're just taking advantage of temporary emotional overreactions. You're buying more when everyone else is running for the exits.

This isn't speculation. It's disciplined opportunism.

The Math Behind Calm Courage

Let's revisit your $10,000 hypothetical investment.

Say you normally invest $100 a day in your ETF portfolio. That's your base rate — your "heartbeat."

Now imagine volatility rises and the VIX hits 35. You increase your daily buy to $150.
A month later, the VIX jumps to 45 — panic everywhere. You calmly raise your daily buy to $200.

If that lasts another month, you've invested more heavily during a downturn, when ETF prices are likely discounted by 10–20%.

Then, when the market stabilizes and the VIX drops back below 25, you return to your base rate of $100 a day.

Over time, this scaling effect lowers your average cost per share, meaning you own more at cheaper prices — while everyone else was paralyzed by fear.

That's how compounding truly accelerates: not through luck, but through courage and consistency.

The Psychology of Doing What Feels Wrong

Here's the hard part:
When volatility spikes and everyone's panicking, your instincts will scream "Stop buying!"

That's normal. It's human.

But remember: when the VIX is high, prices are low.
The market is offering you a sale — a rare opportunity to buy future growth at a discount.

It takes emotional discipline to see that clearly.
Dynamic DCA isn't just a strategy; it's a training tool for your mind. It helps you detach from the crowd's hysteria and act according to logic, not emotion.

You don't need to predict anything. You just need to follow your rules.

A Real-World Perspective

In early 2020, when the pandemic hit, the VIX exploded to nearly 80 — one of the highest readings in history. The market fell over 30% in a few weeks.

Investors who panicked and sold missed one of the fastest recoveries ever.
But those who kept buying — or increased their investments according to volatility — captured massive long-term gains.

Dynamic DCA isn't about timing the bottom. It's about being there — fully and calmly — when the world is too scared to invest.

Fear passes. Quality endures.

The Reward: Sleep and Serenity

The beauty of this method is how emotionally freeing it becomes.

You no longer dread market crashes; you quietly welcome them.

You don't obsess over headlines or predictions; you have a clear system that tells you what to do.

When fear is high, you invest a bit more.

When greed returns, you pull back.

And all along the way, your steady rhythm keeps compounding wealth in the background.

You've turned volatility — once your enemy — into your greatest ally.

Next: How to Put It All on Autopilot

Now that you understand how to use volatility as a compass, the next chapter will show you how to implement Dynamic DCA step-by-step.

We'll walk through automation, cash flow management, and how to "set and forget" your plan so it runs quietly while you live your life.

Because the goal isn't just to grow wealth — it's to do it calmly, intelligently, and automatically.

Chapter 4

The Dynamic DCA Formula — Implementation and Automation

By now, you understand the philosophy behind your strategy. You know what dollar-cost averaging is, how ETFs give you effortless diversification, and how volatility can be turned from an enemy into a friend.

Now it's time to bring it all together — to turn this calm, rational framework into a real-world system that runs quietly in the background of your life.

Because financial peace isn't about constant action — it's about consistent automation.

Step 1: Set Your Base Investment Rhythm

Every dynamic system begins with a baseline.

Ask yourself: How much can I comfortably invest on a consistent basis — daily, weekly, or monthly — without stress?

Let's say your base rate is $100 per day. That's your "heartbeat." It continues rain or shine, up or down, regardless of market noise.

Your base rhythm is sacred — it's what keeps the habit alive.
Whether the VIX is 15 or 45, you're still showing up to the market.

This alone — before any scaling — will already outperform the average investor over time.

Step 2: Define Your Volatility Triggers

Next, you'll link your investment size to the market's emotional state — the VIX.

Here's a simple structure to follow:

VIX Range	Emotion	Multiplier	Daily Investment
12–25	Calm	1×	$100
28–32	Nervous	1.5×	$150
38–42	Fearful	2×	$200
48–52	Panicked	2.5×	$250
60+ Extreme		3× (optional)	$300

When volatility cools down, scale back gradually to your baseline.
For example, if you've been buying $200 daily during a fearful stretch and the VIX drops from 40 to 25, reduce your contribution back to $100.

You're following emotion — but doing it rationally.

Each step up or down has clear rules. There's no guessing, no "gut feeling." It's all about consistency and clarity.

Step 3: Automate Through Your Platform

Now, let's talk about implementation — because your system only works if it's easy to execute.

Some brokers let you automate recurring ETF purchases daily, weekly, or monthly — even for fractional shares.
Here's how:

Choose your ETF (e.g., VTI, VXUS, BND).

Tap "Schedule Reinvestment" or "Recurring Investment."

Set your frequency (daily or weekly).

Enter your base amount ($100 in our example).

To adjust dynamically, you can manually increase or decrease your daily amount based on VIX levels — takes less than a minute.

Tip: You can check the current VIX index anytime by searching "VIX" directly in broker's ticker search bar.

These platforms allow automatic transfers from your bank account into ETFs or mutual funds.
Set up a recurring deposit to your brokerage account, and then schedule purchases on a weekly or biweekly basis.

You can adjust your amounts quarterly or whenever VIX crosses your preset thresholds.

Over time, this becomes effortless — your system runs itself, freeing you from constant monitoring.

Step 4: Manage Your Cash Flow for Flexibility

Dynamic DCA requires a little flexibility — because when fear hits and volatility spikes, you'll want extra cash ready to buy more.

Here's how to prepare:

Keep a small "dry powder" reserve — maybe 10–20% of your investable cash — in a money market fund or high-yield savings account.

When VIX rises into your trigger zones, draw from this reserve to increase your daily buys.

When the market calms down, replenish your reserve by returning to your base contributions.

This way, you're never forced to sell or overextend yourself. You're simply reallocating intelligently.

Step 5: Track Without Obsessing

You don't need to check prices every day. In fact, the less you look, the better.

What you do track are your rules:

Is my base investment continuing as planned?

Has the VIX crossed one of my thresholds?

Am I scaling correctly based on the table?

That's it. No predictions, no news obsession, no emotional roller coaster.

If you want, create a simple spreadsheet or note on your phone:

Base: $100/day

28–32 VIX → $150/day
38–42 VIX → $200/day
48–52 VIX → $250/day
60+ VIX → $300/day

Update it monthly or whenever volatility spikes.

Your only real job is to keep the rhythm going.

A $10,000 Example: Implementation in Action

Let's bring this to life again.

You've got $10,000 ready to invest. You decide to apply the dynamic approach using your base rate of $100 per day.

Here's how it might play out over three market moods:

Period	VIX	Emotion	Investment per Day	Days	Total Invested
Month 1	20	Calm	$100	22	$2,200
Month 2	35	Fear rising	$150	22	$3,300
Month 3	45	Panic	$200	22	$4,400
Total	—	—	—	—	$9,900

By leaning in as volatility rises, you invested more when prices were likely 10–15% lower.
When the market recovers — as it always does eventually — you'll own more shares bought at lower prices.

You didn't predict. You didn't panic. You simply followed your system.

And you still have that extra $100 unspent — because even your math is calm.

Step 6: Let Time and Compounding Do the Rest

The longer you stay in the game, the more powerful this becomes.

Each share you buy at a discount compounds over time. The dividends reinvest. The ETFs appreciate. Volatility smooths out.

You'll look back years later and realize something remarkable:
Your best returns came from the times that felt the worst.

That's not luck — that's the reward for following a rational plan when everyone else was losing their nerve.

Step 7: Live Your Life

This might sound simple, but it's the most important step of all.

Once your system is in place, go live your life.

Don't hover over charts. Don't try to "beat" the market. Don't let the noise invade your peace.

You've built a process that already does the heavy lifting — quietly, automatically, rationally.

That's what financial mastery really looks like: not complexity, but clarity.

IN SUMMARY

Here's what your Dynamic DCA Formula gives you:

A consistent investing habit that never stops.

A clear system for increasing and decreasing your contributions based on volatility.

A portfolio built from 3–4 world-class ETFs.

The ability to sleep peacefully, knowing you're always doing the right thing.

You're no longer reacting to the market — you're dancing with it.

Next: Rebalancing, Risk, and Sleeping Even Better

Now that your system is up and running, we'll move into the next layer of long-term success: rebalancing and risk management.

In the next chapter, you'll learn how to fine-tune your ETF mix once or twice a year, keep your risk profile steady, and continue sleeping well — no matter what the headlines say.

Because the real art of investing isn't just growing wealth — it's protecting your peace.

Chapter 5

Risk, Rebalancing, and Sleeping Well

When you first start investing, it's easy to think that success depends on picking the right moment or finding the perfect fund. But once your Dynamic Dollar-Cost Averaging system is running, you'll realize something deeper: the real challenge isn't building wealth — it's staying calm enough to keep it growing.

In this chapter, we'll talk about managing risk, keeping your portfolio balanced, and maintaining the kind of peace of mind that lets you sleep soundly — even when markets go wild.

THE QUIET POWER OF BALANCE

Every portfolio is like a living ecosystem.
Stocks, bonds, and other assets all play their part. When one grows faster than the others, the balance shifts — sometimes quietly, sometimes dramatically.

That's why even the calmest system needs an occasional adjustment — what investors call rebalancing.

Rebalancing simply means restoring your portfolio to its original proportions.
It's not about predicting the next move — it's about maintaining alignment with your long-term goals.

Why Rebalancing Works

Imagine you start with a simple allocation:

60% in stock ETFs (U.S. + international)

30% in bond ETFs

10% in real estate or dividend ETFs

Over time, your stock ETFs might grow faster than your bonds, shifting your portfolio to, say, 70/25/5.

That's great news — it means stocks have done well — but it also means your portfolio is now riskier than you originally intended.

Rebalancing brings that risk back to your comfort zone by selling a bit of what's grown too much and adding to what's lagged behind.

In other words, it forces you to sell high and buy low, calmly and automatically — the opposite of what most emotional investors do.

How Often Should You Rebalance?

Once or twice a year is plenty.

You can set a simple rule:

Calendar method: Rebalance every 6 or 12 months (e.g., January and July).

Threshold method: Rebalance only if any asset class drifts more than 5–10% from its target allocation.

Either way, the key is consistency, not precision.
The point isn't to react to every little market move — it's to keep your long-term balance intact.

How to Rebalance in Practice

Let's bring this to life with your $10,000 example.

You began with:

$6,000 in stock ETFs

$3,000 in bonds

$1,000 in real estate/dividend ETFs

After a strong year for stocks, your portfolio grows to $12,000, but now looks like this:

Stocks = $8,400 (70%)

Bonds = $2,900 (24%)

Real estate/dividends = $700 (6%)

You simply sell enough stocks to bring them back to 60% of your total, and reinvest that money into bonds and real estate to restore your 60/30/10 balance.

That might mean selling $1,200 worth of stocks and spreading it across the other two categories.

It's mechanical. Emotionless. Rational.
You're maintaining equilibrium, not chasing performance.

Why Rebalancing Is Emotionally Difficult — and Financially Rewarding

When you rebalance, you'll often find yourself trimming the winners and adding to the losers.
That feels unnatural.

Human instinct wants to double down on what's rising and avoid what's falling. But rebalancing turns that instinct on its head — it forces you to buy low and sell high systematically.

This is one of the few ways to guarantee rational behavior in an irrational market.

You'll rarely see short-term results from rebalancing. But over decades, it will smooth your returns, lower your risk, and help you stay invested longer, which is the real secret to compounding.

THE ROLE OF BONDS AND STABILITY

It's tempting to think bonds are boring — and they are, gloriously so.

When the market drops and stock prices tumble, your bond ETFs often rise or at least hold steady. They act as a stabilizer, softening the blows that make other investors panic.

The bond portion of your portfolio isn't about chasing return — it's about protecting your sanity.

And when fear peaks (remember those high VIX moments?), your bond holdings are what let you calmly increase your equity buys without feeling overexposed.

Staying the Course During Storms

The market will test you. That's guaranteed.

There will be stretches when your portfolio feels stuck or when news headlines scream that "this time is different."
It never is.

If you've built your system around:

Regular DCA contributions

A small group of diversified ETFs

Dynamic adjustments based on volatility

Occasional rebalancing to manage risk

Then you've already done everything a rational investor can do. The rest is time and patience.

Remember, the market rewards endurance, not prediction.

Your Portfolio's Personality

One of the most valuable things you'll discover through this process is your true risk tolerance.

Some people can watch a 20% market drop and sleep like a baby. Others lose sleep over a 5% swing.
Neither is right or wrong — but knowing where you stand helps you fine-tune your balance.

If you find yourself anxious during downturns, increase your bond allocation slightly.
If you're too conservative and missing long-term growth, tilt a bit more toward equities.

Your portfolio should reflect not just your goals, but your temperament.

Because peace of mind isn't a luxury — it's a requirement for longevity.

The Emotional Return on Calm Investing

There's a hidden dividend in your Dynamic DCA approach — and it isn't measured in dollars.
It's measured in peace.

You know what you own.
You know how much you invest.
You know when you'll rebalance.
You know how you'll respond to fear.

There's no uncertainty left — just execution.

That's what separates the calm investor from the crowd:
When others are reacting, you're reflecting.
When others are panicking, you're participating.

You've turned money — that old source of stress — into a system that supports your peace of mind.

In Summary

By rebalancing your portfolio once or twice a year, you:

Keep risk at your desired level.

Automatically sell high and buy low.

Maintain your Dynamic DCA system's efficiency.

Protect yourself emotionally from market noise.

Your portfolio stays balanced.
Your strategy stays consistent.
And you stay calm.

That's what it means to sleep well while your wealth grows quietly in the background.

Next: Case Studies — How Calm Wins in the Long Run

In the next chapter, we'll look at historical examples — moments of panic and recovery — to see how your system would have performed during events like 2008, 2020, and 2022.

You'll see, through data and perspective, how the calm investor not only survives volatility but thrives because of it.

Month	VIX	Market Emotion	Daily Buy	Days	Total Invested
1–2	25	Calm	$100	44	$4,400
3	35	Rising fear	$200	22	$4,400
4	50	Panic	$250	22	$5,500
5	45	Fear	$200	22	$4,400
6–10	30–25	Nervous → Calm	$150 → $100	110	$13,500
Total	—	—	—	220	$32,200

Chapter 5.1

Tailoring Your Portfolio to Your Age and Risk Tolerance

So far, we've built the foundation: Dollar-Cost Averaging, ETFs, scaling buys with volatility, and rebalancing to keep your portfolio steady. But one size doesn't fit all. Your ideal portfolio depends on your age and your comfort with risk. After all, you're investing not just to grow money — you're investing so that your future self can sleep soundly.

1. Age as a Guide

A simple principle: the younger you are, the more risk you can take — because time is on your side. Market dips? You can ride them out. Market rallies? You get to compound early.

A classic rule of thumb is:

Stock Allocation (%) = 100 – Your Age
Bond/Stable Allocation (%) = Your Age

Example:

Age	Stocks	Bonds
25	75%	25%
35	65%	35%
45	55%	45%
55	45%	55%
65	35%	65%

This is a starting point — a gentle guide to help you grow when young and protect when older.

2. Adjust for Risk Tolerance

Not everyone can stomach the same swings. Some people wake up in cold sweats if the market drops 10%. Others cheer, seeing opportunity.

Here's a simple framework to align your portfolio with your temperament:

Risk Tolerance	Stocks (%)	Bonds (%)	Notes
Aggressive	80–90	10–20	High growth, high volatility
Moderate	60–70	30–40	Balanced growth and stability
Conservative	40–50	50–60	Lower growth, smoother ride
Very Conservative	20–30	70–80	Focused on capital preservation

Tip: Use your age allocation as a baseline, then tilt it up or down based on how you feel about volatility.

3. Combining Age and Risk

Here's what it might look like in practice:

Age	Aggressive	Moderate	Conservative
25	90/10	80/20	60/40
35	85/15	70/30	50/50
45	80/20	65/35	50/50
55	70/30	55/45	40/60
65	60/40	50/50	30/70

(Stock % / Bond %)

This framework helps you invest in a way that fits your life stage and comfort with risk, making it easier to stick to your system during market turbulence.

4. Applying to Your ETF Portfolio

Let's return to your $10,000 example. Say you're 35 and moderate risk:

Stocks: 70% → $7,000

U.S. Stocks: 60% of stock allocation → $4,200

International Stocks: 40% of stock allocation → $2,800

Bonds: 30% → $3,000

Optional: $0–$1,000 in real estate/dividends

With Dynamic DCA, you invest these amounts gradually, scaling up when volatility spikes. Rebalancing ensures your allocation stays aligned, while age- and risk-based percentages keep your portfolio tailored to your comfort level and life stage.

5. Your Takeaway

Your allocation is a living blueprint, not a static rule. As you age, gain confidence, or experience life changes, your mix may shift. The goal isn't perfection — it's a portfolio you can stick with, no matter how crazy the market gets.

Invest according to your stage of life. Respect your comfort with risk. And let time, discipline, and compounding do the heavy lifting.

Chapter 6

Case Studies and Historical Simulations

Numbers tell stories that words alone cannot. They show how theory becomes reality, how discipline beats panic, and how calm action outperforms emotional reaction.

In this chapter, we'll take your $10,000 investment and simulate how it would have behaved under Dynamic Dollar-Cost Averaging during some of the most turbulent periods in recent market history.

Case Study 1: The 2008 Financial Crisis

The 2008 collapse was catastrophic. Stocks fell over 50% from peak to trough. Fear was everywhere, and the VIX spiked above 80 — one of the highest readings in history.

Let's see how your strategy would have worked:

Base daily buy: $100

VIX 38–42: double buy ($200/day)

VIX 48–52: 2.5× buy ($250/day)

Suppose your $10,000 is deployed over 10 months leading into the crash:
Total invested: $32,200 across the ETF portfolio.

By increasing purchases during high-volatility months, you bought more shares when prices were depressed.
By the end of the crisis, the market recovered gradually — meaning your average cost per share was far lower than a lump-sum investor who had invested at the peak.

The result? A portfolio that compounded faster once recovery began, while the panicked investor was stuck on the sidelines.

Case Study 2: March 2020 — The Pandemic Crash

In March 2020, the market fell nearly 35% in a single month, and the VIX spiked to almost 85. Fear was extreme.

Your Dynamic DCA system would have acted like this:

Base daily buy: $100

VIX 38–42 → $200

VIX 48–52 → $250

VIX 60+ → $300

Period	VIX	Daily Buy	Days	Total Invested
Early Feb	20	$100	20	$2,000
Mid Feb	35	$200	10	$2,000
Early Mar	50	$250	10	$2,500
Mid Mar	80	$300	10	$3,000

Total invested: $9,500 over roughly six weeks.

The market bottomed later in March, and by the end of 2020, the recovery was nearly complete.
Your system ensured you accumulated shares at fire-sale prices, while many investors either panicked or missed the opportunity entirely.

This is the essence of Dynamic DCA: leaning in when others retreat.

Case Study 3: The 2022 Market Correction

2022 was a slower-moving, inflation-driven decline. Stocks dropped 20–25%, bonds dipped, and volatility peaked around 40.

Even though the decline wasn't as dramatic as 2008 or 2020, the Dynamic DCA strategy still worked beautifully:

Daily buy increased by 2× during high VIX periods.

Base contributions continued during calm periods.

Over the course of the year, your $10,000 investment bought more shares at lower prices, creating a stronger foundation for recovery.

The lesson: Dynamic DCA isn't just for crashes — it works in every type of volatility.

Key Lessons from the Simulations

Fear is fuel. The higher the VIX, the more shares you can buy cheaply.

Timing isn't required. You don't need to predict the bottom; your rules do it for you.

Compounding accelerates with volatility. Buying more during fear gives you a lower average cost per share and higher long-term returns.

Peace of mind matters. Dynamic DCA lets you act rationally when everyone else is panicking.

Consistency beats heroics. You don't need to pick stocks, sectors, or trends — you just follow your system.

Visualizing the Power of Calm

Imagine two investors, each starting with $10,000:

Investor A: Lump-sum at the market peak. Panics during crashes, sells, misses rebounds.

Investor B: Uses Dynamic DCA. Increases daily buys during high volatility, stays invested, and rebalances yearly.

Years later, Investor B consistently owns more shares at lower average costs and enjoys higher compounded returns. Investor A, on the other hand, suffers emotional whiplash, frequently underperforms, and struggles to sleep during market stress.

Dynamic DCA turns panic into opportunity. That's the real edge.

PUTTING IT ALL TOGETHER

These case studies prove one central truth: volatility is your friend when you follow a plan.

It's not magic. It's discipline.

It's not prediction. It's participation.
It's not risk-free. It's risk-managed.

By combining:

Dollar-cost averaging

High-quality ETFs

Volatility-based scaling

Annual rebalancing

You've built a system that doesn't just survive crises — it thrives because of them.

Next: The Calm Investor's Mindset

The final chapter will focus on the psychology of long-term investing:

Why sticking to your rules is more important than chasing returns.

How to handle fear, greed, and impatience.

How to turn investing from stress into a source of confidence and peace.

After all, the goal isn't just wealth — it's sleeping well while your money works for you.

Chapter 7

The Calm Investor's Mindset

B y now, you've seen the strategy, the math, and the historical evidence. You understand Dollar-Cost Averaging, ETFs, volatility, Dynamic scaling, and rebalancing. You've watched $10,000 evolve in simulations through fear, panic, and recovery.

But there's one final piece that determines whether this system truly works: your mind.

Because investing isn't just numbers — it's emotion, behavior, and habit. And the calm investor knows that mastering the mind is just as important as mastering the market.

The Most Powerful Asset: Emotional Discipline

The stock market is a machine that rewards rational, patient, and consistent behavior — and punishes emotion, impatience, and panic.

Your Dynamic DCA system is a tool to help you act rationally, even when the world is irrational. But tools alone aren't enough. You must develop emotional discipline:

Ignore the headlines. The news thrives on fear and drama. You don't.

Trust the process. You have a system built on logic and history — follow it.

Detach from short-term movements. Prices move daily. Your goal is growth over years, not days.

This is why even sophisticated investors fail — not from lack of knowledge, but from lack of control. Emotional discipline is what separates the calm investor from the crowd.

Fear Is Your Ally

Remember the VIX? That measure of fear in the market?

For most, high volatility triggers panic. For you, it's a buying signal.

The calm investor reframes fear: it's not a warning to flee. It's an invitation to participate. The higher the fear, the greater the opportunity.

VIX 28–32 → increase your daily buy by 50%

VIX 38–42 → double your buy

VIX 48–52 → 2.5× your buy

This approach doesn't rely on predicting the bottom. It relies on logic, rules, and courage. When everyone else is running, you're quietly buying the foundations of future wealth.

PATIENCE: THE INVISIBLE FORCE

Nothing grows instantly.
Not crops, not careers, not wealth.

Compounding works silently. Shares purchased at fear-induced discounts will reward you — eventually.

The calm investor knows this and embraces time as an ally. You invest consistently. You rebalance periodically. You scale into volatility. And you let time do the heavy lifting.

The emotional payoff? You sleep better. You no longer wake up at 3 a.m., obsessing over charts and headlines. You've built a system that works — so you can live life without constant stress.

Avoiding the Comparison Trap

One of the most destructive forces for investors is envy: comparing your results to others.

Someone else bought a hot stock and doubled their money.

Another trader "timed" the market perfectly.

It's irrelevant. The calm investor doesn't chase. They participate steadily, knowing that consistent, rule-based investing always beats emotional heroics in the long run.

Your success is measured by your consistency, your peace of mind, and your long-term results — not by daily market chatter.

THE RITUAL OF INVESTING CALMLY

Turn investing into a ritual:

Check the VIX weekly or daily, depending on your plan.

Adjust your contribution according to the Dynamic DCA table.

Invest automatically through your chosen ETFs.

Rebalance periodically, once or twice a year.

Step back and let compounding work quietly.

That's it. Minimal effort, maximum impact, maximum peace.

The Real Wealth Is Peace of Mind

Money can buy security, comfort, and opportunity. But money gained while losing sleep, panicking daily, or second-guessing every decision is no wealth at all.

Dynamic DCA is powerful because it aligns financial growth with emotional calm. You're not just growing your money — you're cultivating patience, courage, and clarity.

When the market crashes tomorrow — or in ten years — you will remain calm, because your system is designed to thrive during fear, not crumble under it.

YOUR TAKEAWAY

To summarize the calm investor's mindset:

Follow the rules. Your system is your shield.

Buy more when others panic. Fear is fuel.

Rebalance to maintain alignment. Don't let success create hidden risk.

Let compounding and time work quietly.

Protect your peace of mind. Wealth is meaningless without serenity.

This is how $10,000 invested thoughtfully today can grow into financial independence tomorrow — all while you sleep well at night.

FINAL THOUGHT

The market will always move. Volatility will always appear. Headlines will always scream.

The calm investor does not fight these realities — they flow with them.
They invest steadily, scale intelligently, rebalance wisely, and above all, trust the process.

Your wealth is built not by chasing every trend or timing every dip, but by showing up consistently, acting rationally, and keeping fear in its proper place.

Invest calmly. Sleep well. Let time and discipline do the rest.

About the Author

I've spent my career in the heart of the financial markets — first as a stockbroker, then as a trader. I've seen the thrill of a soaring market and the gut-wrenching panic when everything falls apart.

One moment that left a lasting mark on me was the 1987 market crash. Stocks plunged seemingly without warning, and fear overtook reason. I watched countless investors, many of them seasoned, liquidate their portfolios at rock-bottom prices — wiping out years of careful savings in a matter of days. It was heartbreaking, but it also taught me one of the most important lessons in investing: the market punishes emotion and rewards discipline.

Since then, I've dedicated myself to finding ways to help everyday investors stay calm, stay consistent, and harness the power of markets — even when fear is at its peak. I've studied decades of data, refined strategies, and developed methods like Dynamic Dollar-Cost Averaging so that investors can sleep at night, grow steadily, and avoid the mistakes that devastate so many during market panics.

This book is the culmination of those lessons. It's practical, motivational, and grounded in real experience — not just theory. My goal is simple: to help you invest with confidence, act rationally when others panic, and turn volatility into opportunity.

Remember: wealth isn't just numbers in a portfolio — it's peace of mind, long-term growth, and the freedom to live your life without fear of the market.